Microsoft®
Access for Office 365
Beginning
Instructor Guide

COPYRIGHT

TRADEMARKS

DISCLAIMER

Product Code: MS ACCESS 365-1 GUIDE 19.01

TABLE OF CONTENTS

DEVELOPMENT PHILOSOPHY

As an experienced instructor, you have probably taught from many training manuals, each developed/written in a different manner. Each developer has a distinct way of approaching a class and we are, of course, no different.

Our number one concern is to return control of the classroom to the <u>instructor</u>. Most of the training manuals written are oriented towards a "tutorial" format, requiring the instructor to strictly follow a script. If you deviate from the script or skip a section, the end results do not always match the exercise, which throws the students off. Or the follow-up exercises depended on you completing the previous exercise exactly as specified in order to work.

As a result, the trainer simply becomes a "reader" - meaning you end up reading the exercise almost word-for-word to the student. As long as students can read, they really don't need you unless <u>they</u> deviate from the script and get into trouble.

If you do skip a section or change things around, students get irritated because "that's not the way it is in the book!" Your class is actually being taught by the training manual and <u>not</u> by you!

We believe that **you**, not the manual should be controlling the flow of the class. After all, you are the professional being paid for the training! Every experienced instructor has their own way of teaching a class. You know what exercises are good examples, when to give them and how long to spend on a topic. If a class is slower or faster, you can sense that and can give more exercises as needed or maybe spend a little more time on a topic if the class is a bit slower.

Our courseware is written in the form of a "reference" manual - meaning that the students can use the manual when they return to work/home as a reference rather than a step-by-step tutorial.

Think back for a moment to one of your recent classes where you were teaching from a tutorial manual. Remember that student sitting in the back, not paying attention to a single word you were saying? What was he/she doing? They were reading ahead in the manual, doing every little step in the book as fast as they could read and type! They were so pleased with themselves that they could "read" how to do this program that they missed out on all your great examples, tricks/shortcuts and additional explanations! This happens all of the time with scripted courses. These people don't really learn this way, they just blindly type in commands, not really understanding what they are doing.

This is only one of the many problems that you run into with "tutorial" courseware, but let's focus on the advantages of using our manuals.

ADVANTAGES

There are several advantages to using this format which we have broken down according to three basic categories: students; instructors; and clients.

Advantages for the Student

➤ It's an easy-to-read reference guide. If a student needs to know how to do something, they don't have to read through pages and pages of "Johnny's" letter to mom to figure it out!

Once students leave your class and are dependent upon themselves, they need something that they can use to quickly look up a command or function. Our manual discusses each major topic on a separate page in an easy-to-follow format.

➤ Student notes are in the same book - not written on some pad of paper that they just grabbed for class and will misplace later! How many times have you seen students leave their notes in class after writing down all of the information? But how many manuals are left behind?

The left page of our manual is set aside for the student to be able to write down in their own words what they understand and also any additional information that you might be giving. And it can be written right across from the page of the topic actually being referred to, making it easy to refer back to once class has ended.

➤ Each course can be tailored to the class.   Some of the sample exercises in tutorials are so boring or have absolutely nothing in common with the client. Without predefined exercises, you can tailor the course to the client using your examples that you have developed over the years.

Advantages for the Instructor

➢ Students pay attention. Since they do not really know what you are going to be doing next, students have to follow your instructions. This keeps you in control of the class instead of having students in different parts of the book.

➢ You can alter the speed of the course as required. As you know, each class progresses differently depending on the various experience levels of the students. If you find you have a faster group, you can give additional exercises or go into more depth for each topic. If you have a slower class, you are not pressured into having to complete all of the "scenarios" or "practice" exercises if you feel you cannot cover them adequately.

Again, you are in control. You can speed up or slow the class down as you see fit. You can expand or condense the amount of information covered on a topic as required.

➢ You can customize your courses without having to do all the development work! Simply change the exercises to topics that relate more closely to the client. This makes them feel as if you are "customizing" the course for them! We have supplied all of our exercise pages in a separate "Files" folder which may be modified and included with the manuals as the training company sees fit.

Advantages for the Client

> The client is assured of having qualified instructors. Since there are no step-by-step "follow me" type instructions, the instructor must really know the material. How many times have you heard from other instructors how they "winged" it through class by reading the manual? It doesn't take much for someone who does not know the program well to still "teach" a course if they have a step-by-step tutorial to follow!
>
> Would you send that instructor to one of <u>your</u> clients?

> More productive employees. Since students <u>actually</u> have to pay attention, students absorb more of what they do.
>
> Since the class can be customized, the client can be sure that students are learning exactly what they need in order to perform their jobs more efficiently once they return to their workplace.

HOW TO USE THIS MANUAL

This manual was designed to be used as a reference. It covers each topic discussed in class in the order they will be introduced.

This is not a step-by-step tutorial. Our feeling is that you did not pay to have someone stand in front of class and <u>read</u> you something that you could do on your own. Through our own classroom experience, we have discovered that students don't read detailed descriptions and that lengthy text is ignored. They prefer to explore and try things out.

In typical tutorials, students often get lost following rote procedures and get caught in error conditions from which they can't back out of. Besides, once students leave class, they just want something where they can look up a subject quickly without having to read through an entire tutorial.

Keys and commands that you need to press are displayed as icons such as `ENTER` or `↑`.

Each topic starts on a new page, making things easy to find and follow. Any keyboard shortcuts will be included within the TIP boxes while mouse shortcuts will always include the MOUSE icon beside it.

The next page shows how a typical topic will be discussed and each part found in the book.

THE TOPIC TITLE WILL BE ON TOP

USAGE:

This part of the manual explains what the command is used for, how it works and other miscellaneous information.

This icon indicates tools or buttons to click on with your mouse.

This part lists the keystrokes and function keys the user may press as a shortcut way of performing the command.

Microsoft Access supports a whole host of touch-screen gestures, including the swiping, pinching and rotating motions familiar to smartphone and tablet users. Tapping an item opens it; pressing and holding an item pops up a menu to display more information about it (similar to [RIGHT] clicking). This icon indicates a touch-screen gesture.

> **NOTE:** *This box will tell of things to watch out for. The symbol in the left column always indicates an important note to remember.*

> **TIP:** *This box will let you in on a little secret or shortcut when working with Access. When you see this icon, you'll know that a "TIP is available.*

Module One

- **Database Basics**
- **Running Access**
- **The Initial Screen**
- **Opening a Database**
- **Working with Help**

DATABASE BASICS

A database is a collection of information, just as your address book is a collection of data. Whenever you access the database, whether it is to add new information, get information, change information, or sort the information into some meaningful order, you are **managing** the database.

A computer database management system, like Access, performs these types of operations on a database that is stored on a computer disk. It allows you to add, change, delete, look up and sort information. However, tasks that may take the computer only a few seconds to perform may take you several minutes, hours, or even days.

Paper databases are referred to as **files**. When using the computer, however, we refer to them as either **files** or **tables**, depending on the program. Access calls them tables. The term tables stems from the unique design that all databases use. Every table within a database is organized in columns and rows.

Suppose you have an address book. Each entry in the book contains the name, address and phone number of an individual. The entry contains four lines of information: (1) Name, (2) address, (3) city, state, zipcode, and (4) phone number, as illustrated in the example below:

```
Samantha Stevens
1640 Morning Glory Circle
Salem, MA  23555
(212)444-6666

Fred & Wilma Flintstone
33 Granite Grove
Bedrock, CA  92617
(714)777-8900
```

Each entry in the book would be listed in Access on a single line and would be called a **record**. Each unique piece of information within the record (name, address, city/state/zip, and phone) would be separated by column and referred to as a **field**.

Name	**Address**	**City/State/Zip**	**Phone**
Sam Stevens	1640 M.G.	Salem, MA 23555	(212) 444-6666
Fred Flintstone	33 Granite Grove	Bedrock, CA 92617	(714) 777-8900

Tables, then, consist of columns (fields) and rows (records).

Tables can be used to store any kind of information - inventory, bookkeeping, accounts payable, receivables and just about anything else that might come to mind.

When storing information within a database table, each piece of data must be stored under a unique field name. This will be discussed in greater detail later in the manual, under the section of creating a table within Access.

RUNNING MICROSOFT ACCESS

USAGE:

Access can be launched through the Windows desktop, the Start menu or the taskbar (located along the bottom of the desktop window).

If you have pinned a shortcut to your desktop, click or tap the **Access** icon to run the application.

If you have pinned it to your taskbar, click on the Access icon:

If Access isn't pinned to your desktop or taskbar, you'll need to open it through the Start menu.

 Open the Start menu.

Instructor Note:

After offering a brief overview of databases, have students access the program.

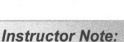

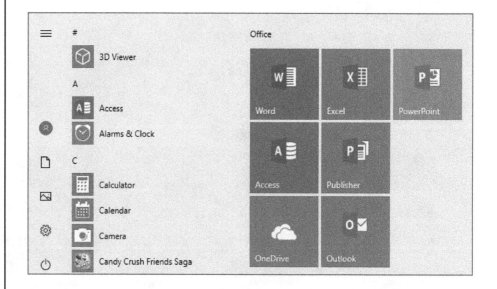

If it isn't already pinned to the Start menu (along the right), scroll through the alphabetical listing of installed apps or click on a letter to display an alphabetical index where you can quickly get to the app based on the first letter of its name.

THE OPENING SCREEN

When you first run the app, you'll be presented with the following screen:

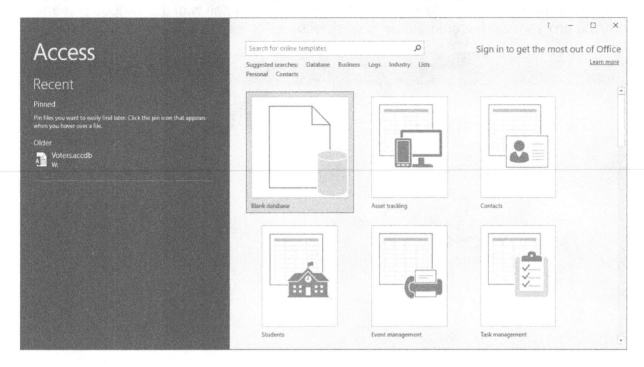

If you've already been working with Access, you can use the left portion of the window to open recently used databases (which are automatically displayed in that section for easy access).

Using the right portion of the window, you can create a new database based on of the many templates available. If you don't see a template that matches the database you want to create, you can search for one online. To create your own custom database and not use any of Access' templates, simply select the "Blank desktop database" option.

If you chose to create a blank database, you'll need to assign a name to it:

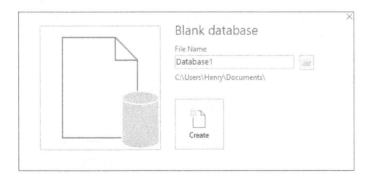

Select where you want to store the new database, assign a name to it and then click on this button.

THE INITIAL ACCESS SCREEN

The screen can be a bit intimidating the first time you see it as there are so many items displayed. However, if you take a few minutes to familiarize yourself with the various screen elements, the program will become easier to work with.

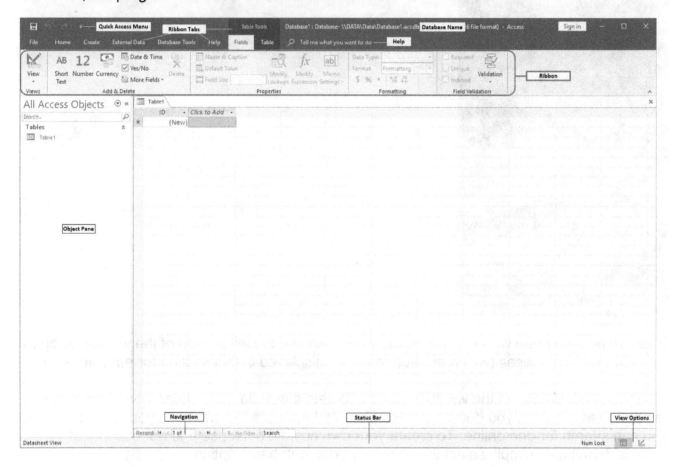

Along the top left corner of the screen is **Save** tool as well as the **Undo** and **Redo** tools.

Since those are tools that are most often used, they are placed in a convenient location on what is referred to as the "Quick Access Toolbar". Click or tap on the button to the right of these tools ▼ to customize this Quick Access Toolbar.

The name of current database is displayed in the middle. A generic name is given to each new database you create (**Database1**).

 If you are going to collaborate with other users, you will need to sign in to your Microsoft account so that you can share the database with others.

 The upper right side of the screen contains three icons for minimizing, maximizing, and closing the program.

Instructor Note:

This screen will take several minutes to discuss in detail – do not go too quickly over each of the sections.

The second line contains tabs which are used to access a series of **Ribbons** to help you quickly find the commands needed to complete a task. Commands are organized in logical groups that are collected together under these tabs. Each tab relates to a type of activity.

The last item on the ribbon (a magnifying glass $\mathcal{P}$ with the words "***Tell me what you want to do..***") is an expansive help feature, offering immediate access to functions and actions within Access.

To collapse the ribbon, press CTRL + F1. Press CTRL + F1 a second time to display the ribbon again. Even while collapsed, clicking or tapping on a tab will display the ribbon for that tab.

Touch screen users can also display an additional set of commonly used buttons down the right side of the screen (on what is referred to as the **Touch Bar**). To display the Touch Bar, click or tap on ▼ (on the Quick Access Toolbar) and select Touch/Mouse Mode from the pull-down menu. This will also increase the space between buttons on the ribbon.

Use the ALT key to access the ribbon directly from the keyboard. For example, if you were to press ALT + C, you could access the "Create" Ribbon. Each time you press ALT, Access displays corresponding letters for the ribbon items to help you to continue using keyboard shortcuts to select them.

Down the left side of the screen is the **Object Pane** which allows you to work on specific database items.

The bottom of the screen includes the navigation area and the **Status Bar** (located at the very bottom of the screen). The status bar displays the current view along with messages regarding the currently displayed table or form.

If you are viewing one of the database objects (such as a table), towards the right side of the status bar are the **View Icons**. For example, datasheet view is best for editing the data within the table while design view is used when editing the structure of the table.

WORKING WITH HELP

USAGE:

Access has an expansive Help feature, offering quick and extensive help without you having to do more than enter the item you need help on.

Using the **Tell me** search bar, simply enter the function or feature you're looking for and Access will offer the function itself (rather than a help page describing it).

Click or tap in this section (located to the right of the ribbons) and type your question.

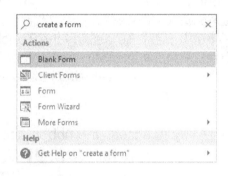

As soon as you begin typing, Access will display help on that topic.

If Access finds the related commands for that topic, it displays them in the pull-down menu.

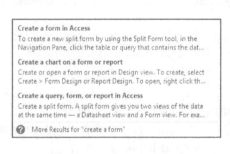

If none of the commands listed are what you want, click on the "Get Help on…" item for an additional menu containing more detailed information on the topic you are searching for.

Clicking on one of the items within the "Get Help on …" submenu displays a new panel along the right side of your screen:

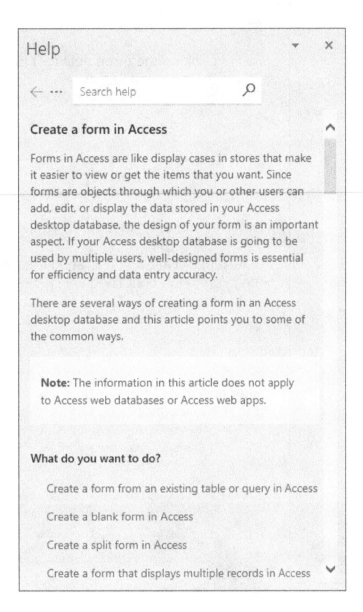

This panel displays help on the item you selected.

Scroll through the step-by-step instructions and diagrams.

The article may include links to related help topics. Some links may require Internet access as they will attempt to launch your Internet browser and access Microsoft's support website.

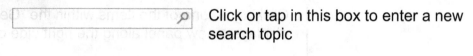 Click or tap in this box to enter a new search topic

← Click on this arrow to return to the previous help screen.

… Click on the three dots (…) to display a pull-down menu with the following items:

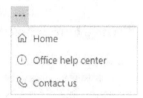

At the end of each help topic, you will see two items:

One item will allow you to send feedback to Microsoft as to whether the information contained within the help panel was helpful:

Was this information helpful?

| Yes | No |

After answering the question, you can also include a comment as part of the feedback you are sending Microsoft:

Great! Any other feedback?

To protect your privacy, please do not include contact information in your feedback. Review our privacy policy.

| Send | No thanks |

The second item (at the bottom of the help panel) allows you to launch your Internet browser and view more detailed information on the currently selected topic through Microsoft's support website:

Read article in browser

You can then use your browser's print option if you'd like to print out information on the selected topic.

EXITING HELP

✖ Click or tap this button (located in the top right corner) to **close** the help window and return to your database.

SCREENTIPS

A common problem most users encounter is not knowing what each tool on the screen represents.

For example, the SAVE tool is displayed as a 3.5" diskette which some users do not immediately relate to saving a file.

To alleviate this problem, Access offers quick mouse assistance on each tool, referred to as ScreenTips.

As you point to a tool, Access will display a quick note as to the tool's function.

After Delete

Create logic that runs after a record has been deleted.

Use [Old].[Field Name] to inspect the value of a field before the record was deleted.

Module Two

- Viewing a Table
- Navigating
- Editing
- Working with AutoCorrect
- Spell Checking
- Table vs Form View

VIEWING A TABLE

USAGE:

A table is a collection of information stored in columns and rows. It looks very much like a spreadsheet in Excel.

To look at the contents of a table, you must open the table you want to view.

If the tables are not being displayed, click or tap on this pull-down (located along the left side of the screen).

Instructor Note:

The next two pages discuss the Datasheet View options and how to navigate through a table.

Be sure to offer plenty of time so that students feel comfortable.

Access opens a new window for the table. This columnar view is referred to as the **Datasheet View**, as indicated in the left corner of the status bar.

The datasheet view will be displayed:

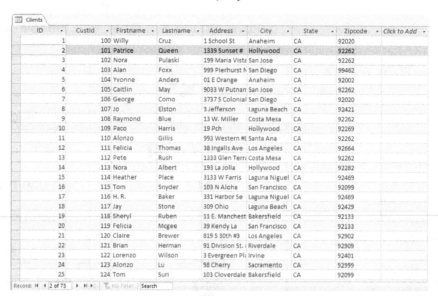

ID	CustId	Firstname	Lastname	Address	City	State	Zipcode	Click to Add
1	100	Willy	Cruz	1 School St	Anaheim	CA	92020	
2	101	Patrice	Queen	1339 Sunset #	Hollywood	CA	92262	
3	102	Nora	Pulaski	199 Maria Vista	San Jose	CA	92262	
4	103	Alan	Foxx	999 Pierhurst N	San Diego	CA	99462	
5	104	Yvonne	Anders	01 E Orange	Anaheim	CA	92002	
6	105	Caitlin	May	9033 W Putnan	San Jose	CA	92262	
7	106	George	Como	3737 S Colonial	San Diego	CA	92020	
8	107	Jo	Elston	3 Jefferson	Laguna Beach	CA	92421	
9	108	Raymond	Blue	13 W. Miller	Costa Mesa	CA	92262	
10	109	Paco	Harris	19 Pch	Hollywood	CA	92269	
11	110	Alonzo	Gillis	993 Western #8	Santa Ana	CA	92262	
12	111	Felicia	Thomas	38 Ingalls Ave	Los Angeles	CA	92664	
13	112	Pete	Rush	1333 Glen Terra	Costa Mesa	CA	92262	
14	113	Nora	Albert	193 La Jolla	Hollywood	CA	92282	
15	114	Heather	Place	3133 W Farris	Laguna Niguel	CA	92469	
16	115	Tom	Snyder	103 N Aloha	San Francisco	CA	92099	
17	116	H. R.	Baker	331 Harbor Se	Laguna Niguel	CA	92469	
18	117	Jay	Stone	309 Ohio	Laguna Beach	CA	92429	
19	118	Sheryl	Ruben	11 E. Manchest	Bakersfield	CA	92133	
20	119	Felicia	Mcgee	39 Kendy La	San Francisco	CA	92133	
21	120	Claire	Brewer	819 S 30th #3	Los Angeles	CA	92902	
22	121	Brian	Herman	91 Division St. :	Riverdale	CA	92909	
23	122	Lorenzo	Wilson	3 Evergreen Pla	Irvine	CA	92401	
24	123	Alonzo	Lu	98 Cherry	Sacramento	CA	92999	
25	124	Tom	Suri	103 Cloverdale	Bakersfield	CA	92099	

Record: I◄ ◄ 2 of 73 ► ►I ►⊞ No Filter Search

If you have more than one table open, each will be in its own tab. You can then switch between the two tables by clicking on the appropriate tab.

The status bar (located beneath the datasheet) also displays the current record and the total number of records within the table so that you can easily move between them.

☐ If the program is not taking up the full screen, you may want to click or tap on the **Maximize** button (located in the upper right corner of the Access window) to take full advantage of the screen and view more records.

If there are more fields (columns) than can fit across the window, you will see a scroll bar along the bottom right side of the window. Use this scroll bar to scroll to the right (or left) for additional fields.

MOVING AROUND WITHIN THE TABLE

To move around in a table, use the following keys:

KEYS	RESULT
TAB or →	One field to the right
SHIFT + TAB or ←	One field to the left
↑	Up one record
↓	Down one record
PG↑	Up one screenful
PG↓	Down one screenful
CTRL + HOME	Beginning of the table
CTRL + END	End of the table
HOME	First field of the current record
END	Last field of the current record

Instructor Note:

Be sure to discuss the shortcut keys and then allow ample practice time.

To move to a field using the mouse, simply click on it.

NOTE:	You can also use the scroll wheel on your mouse to quickly move up and down through your database.

You can also use the navigation buttons located in the lower left corner of the table.

| | Moves to the **next** record |

| | Moves to the **previous** record |

| | Moves to the **first** record |

| | Moves to the **last** record |

| | Moves to the end of the form or datasheet and adds a new record. |

Instructor Note:

Be sure students also have time to practice with the navigation buttons.

| `6` | If you click or tap in the record number box, you can type a record number you want to go to. |

This is the **Vertical Scroll Bar** (located along the right side of the window) which can be used to move through the table records when you cannot see all of the records within the table.

Record: 18 of 73   If you drag the scroll box up/down, Access will display the current record number. This is useful for navigating through very large tables.

PRACTICE EXERCISE

Instructions:	❶	Open the **Sample** database.
	❷	Open the **Clients** table.
	❸	Practice moving around within the table to become familiar with the different parts.

EDITING A TABLE

USAGE:

When you first open a table, Access places your cursor in the first field and highlights the data. If you begin typing, the highlighted data is replaced by the characters you type. Be sure to move the cursor before typing or all of the highlighted information will be replaced by your typing.

To edit another field, click or tap in the field you want to edit.

If you prefer using the keyboard:

[F2]

You are automatically placed in "insert" mode, meaning that any text you type is added to the existing data.

To cancel your changes, press [ESC] once to restore the current field, press [ESC] again to restore the record. Make sure you cancel the changes <u>before</u> you move to another record since Access saves your changes when you move away from the current record.

> **NOTE:** *If you do move to another record, immediately use the* **↺▾** *tool to undo the last action. Remember that the UNDO feature only undoes the last action within Access and not all actions can be reversed!*

While working in the table, you may see the following icons located in the left-most column (called the record selector column):

     🖉   Indicates you are editing the record.

     ✳   Indicates a new record.

> **NOTE:** *You cannot edit counter fields, calculated fields, locked/disabled fields, or fields in locked records.*

The following table lists keys and their functions while editing:

KEYS	RESULT
CTRL +;	Inserts current date.
CTRL + :	Inserts current time.
CTRL + ALT + SPACEBAR	Inserts default value.
CTRL + "	Duplicates the data from the same field of the previous record.
CTRL + ENTER	Inserts a new line for the field.
CTRL + ➕	Adds a new record to the end of the table.
CTRL + ➖	Deletes the current record. You will be asked to confirm the deletion.
ESC	Undoes the editing performed on a field (before you leave the record).
ESC ESC	Undoes the editing performed on a record (before you leave the record).

Instructor Note:

Some students feel comfortable using keyboard shortcuts so always include them in your discussion and demonstration.

To quickly add a new record to the bottom of your table, click or tap on 🔽 (located along the bottom of the datasheet view).

There are also two buttons within the **Records** section on the Home Ribbon to add/remove a record, as shown below:

📋 New   **Adds** a new record. You will be taken to a blank record at the end of the table.

✕ Delete ▾   **Deletes** a record. You will be asked to confirm the record deletion.

USING AUTOCORRECT

USAGE:

Access has a feature referred to as **AutoCorrect**. This feature will correct your common spelling mistakes <u>as</u> you type. Not only will it check your spelling, it can also detect incorrect capitalization at the beginning of words (HEllo) and correct other mistakes.

To set AutoCorrect options:

Open the **File Ribbon** and select Options (located towards the bottom of the list).

Select the **Proofing** options, which will display the following box:

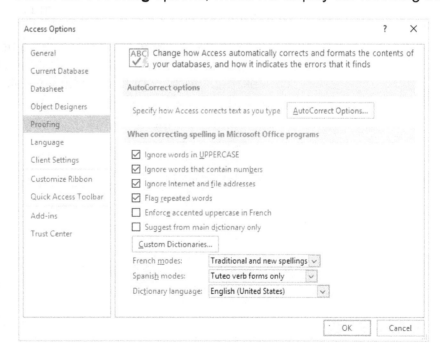

Instructor Note:

Show the students how to add their own words to the dictionary.

However, once a word has been added, be sure they then delete it so that no permanent changes are made on the training systems.

The bottom portion of the box contains spell checking options while the top portion contains AutoCorrect items.

Click or tap AutoCorrect Options... to open a second window.

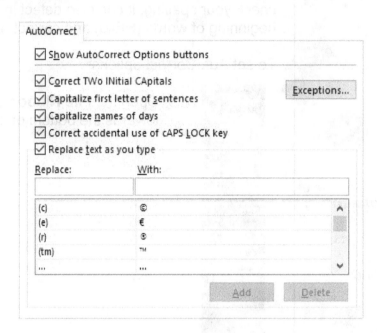

Access provides a list of the most common misspelled words and abbreviations. If you scroll through the list, you will see many of the words that you have probably abused at one time or another.

You can specify any exceptions to make when correcting words.

The checkboxes at the top of the dialog box allow you to enable/disable such choices as automatically correcting two capitalized letters, capitalizing the first letter of each sentence, capitalizing any days entered, and automatically correcting mistakes made by leaving the CAPS LOCK key on.

ADDING WORDS TO AUTOCORRECT

If you feel that there are still a few more words that you typically have trouble with, you can add them to the list so AutoCorrect can catch them in the future by following the steps outlined below:

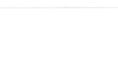

❶   Type the common mistake in the **Replace:** section.

❷   Type the correctly spelled word in the **With:** section.

❸   Once you have reviewed the spelling, click or tap [Add].

Check the **Replace text as you type** box if you would like Access to make the replacements as you work.

REMOVING WORDS FROM AUTOCORRECT

If you need to remove an item from the list, scroll through the list and click on the item to remove. Once the item is highlighted, click or tap on [Delete].

REPLACING EXISTING ENTRIES

If you feel that an existing entry needs to be replaced with another correction, select the entry from the list, make your changes to it and then click or tap on [Replace].

When done with this dialog box, click or tap on [OK].

USING THE SPELL CHECKER

USAGE:

Instructor Note:

Explain the importance of spell checking a table before creating and printing forms and reports.

Access also has a built-in spell checker that should be used on a periodic basis to check the spelling in your tables to avoid any embarrassing mistakes! Although it can be used anytime, the most important time is before you print the table or show it to others!

ABC ✓ Spelling   Click or tap on the **Spelling** tool (located within the **Records** section on the Home Ribbon).

The following dialog box will be displayed:

Access stops at the first unrecognized word and highlights it. The spell checker will try to find words that come close to the unrecognized word and list them in the **Suggestions** section.

If you don't see the correct word right away, you may be able to scroll through the list using the scroll bar, as shown below:

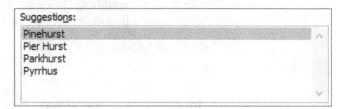

The following buttons are provided within the spell-checking panel:

Instructor Note:

Offer a few examples of words that users may wish to add to their custom dictionary (such as business names and acronyms).

Ignore Ignore All	If the word should remain as it is, select the **Ignore** button. Access also offers the option of **Ignore All** if the word in question appears throughout the table.
Add	If the word should be added to your custom dictionary for future reference, click or tap on this button.
Change Change All	If one of the suggestions is correct, double-click or double-tap on the correct spelling or highlight the word and choose the **Change** button. If you are afraid you misspelled a word more than once, click on the **Change All** button.
AutoCorrect	Use this button to add the word to the AutoCorrect list. In the future, when you misspell this word while typing, Access will automatically correct it - without you having to access the spell checker.

Instructor Note:

Even though this box is a bit overwhelming, be sure to cover each and every option within it.

The "check spelling as you type" feature is one of the most important since most users want that turned on.

Click or tap on Options... to access the following dialog box:

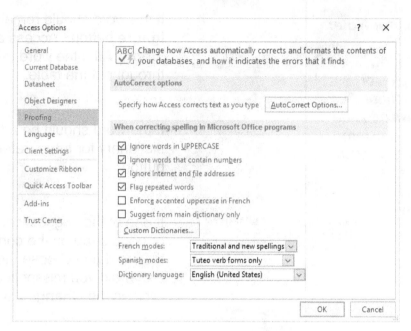

The box is divided into two main sections. The top section is used to specify AutoCorrect options while the bottom section defines how spelling corrections will be made.

Dictionary language   Click or tap on the down arrow ⊡ beside this option to specify the language you want to use while spellchecking. The right section of the box allows you to set language-specific options.

NOTE:	By default, Access does not check words that are in all uppercase (due to acronyms). If you tend to type in uppercase, you will need to remove the checkmark from the option labeled "Ignore words in UPPERCASE".

When done setting the options, click or tap on OK .

When the spell check is complete, a confirmation box appears. Click or tap OK to confirm you are done with the spell checker.

PRACTICE EXERCISE

Instructions:	❶	View the **Clients** table.
	❷	Edit the table to delete record #5.
	❸	Change record #1 so that the zip code is 90207.
	❹	Delete the street address from record #2.
	❺	Undo the last editing change (the field deletion).
	❻	Spell Check the **City** field and make the necessary corrections.

FORM VS TABLE VIEW

USAGE:

You can work with forms in Access as well as tables. While a table shows a screenful of records, a form displays all of the information for one record at a time. A form record is equivalent to one row of information in a table. You may find it easier while editing to view only one record at a time rather than viewing the entire table listing. Forms can be customized to show totals, graphics, and other specialized features. You can easily design a form to approximate an existing paper form, making data entry more familiar to users.

Forms consist of "controls" that represent fields, labels, lines, rectangles and other design objects.

OPENING A FORM

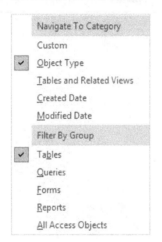

To open an existing form, click or tap on this pull-down list (which is located along the left side of the database window). Access will display all available database objects. If you don't see all of the objects, enable Object Type.

Choose "Forms" to display which forms have been associated with the current database.

From the list of forms, select the one you want to work with.

The following diagram is a sample form:

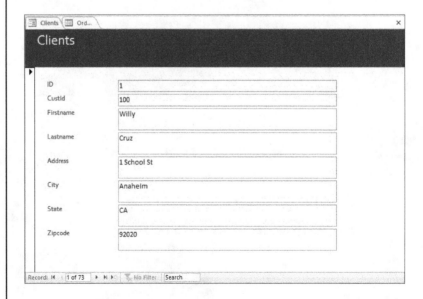

SWITCHING VIEWS

View

While in Form view, if you click or tap on the bottom portion of this button you will be able to choose from three viewing options:

Instructor Note:

Have students try out each of the views.

Form View   This view returns you to form view if you have chosen to switch to layout or design view.

Layout View   This view adds a new ribbon across the top of the screen (labeled Format) which allows you to fully customize the form. It's the most intuitive view for form modification because you can see the data as you are customizing it.

Design View   This final view offers a more detailed view of the form's structure. You can see the header, footer, and detail sections for the form. However, you can't actually see the data while you are making changes in this view.

If you want to see multiple records on the screen, you can always choose to view the table again. If the table is still open, click or tap the tab representing the table (towards the top of the screen).

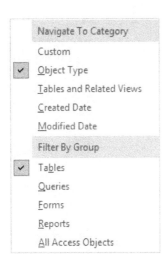

If the table has been closed, click or tap this pull-down list (which is located along the left side of the database window). Access will display all available database objects. Choose "Tables" to display which tables have been associated with the current database.

From the list of tables, select the one you want to work with.

PRACTICE EXERCISE

Instructions:	❶	Open the **Clients** and **Orders** table.
	❷	Open the **Orders** form.
	❸	Switch between the various views for each table.
	❹	While viewing the "Clients" table, change the city "Anaheim" to "Anaheim Hills" for Record #1.
	❺	Undo the change.

Module Three

- Resizing the Table
- Resizing a Column
- Moving a Column
- Hiding/Unhiding Columns
- Freezing/Unfreezing Columns
- Changing Fonts & Row Height
- Sorting the Data
- Printing the View

CHANGING THE TABLE IMAGE

USAGE:

Instructor Note:

If students have worked with Excel, this portion should go fairly fast since the next few pages contain actions that are quite similar.

When working in the datasheet view, you have several options for customizing the view to suit your needs.

SIZING THE ACCESS WINDOW

If Access is not taking up the entire screen, you can adjust the window size, as shown below:

⇔ ⇕ ⬉ ⬈   To customize the size, move to one of the window's borders. Mouse users will notice that the pointer changes into a two-sided arrow. Drag to resize the window.

☐   Click or tap on this button to maximize the window.

CHANGING COLUMN WIDTH

You may at some point be viewing a table that has too many fields to fit on the screen at once. While editing or viewing, switching back and forth between the columns can become irritating. Access allows you to change the column size while viewing a table so that you can fit more columns on the screen. Of course, changing column size may also be needed if a column is too narrow or wide.

Point to the right of the column header to be changed. Mouse users will notice that the pointer changes to a double-sided arrow. Drag the column to the desired width. Remember you are only changing the column size while viewing the table; you are not changing the actual field size.

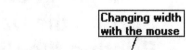

Changing width with the mouse

Customer Id:	Firstname:	⇔	Lastname:
100	WILLY		CRUZ
101	PATRICE		QUEEN
102	NORA		PULASKI
103	ALAN		FOXX

TIP:	**Double-click** *when you see the double-arrow to adjust the size to fit the longest column entry!*

MOVING A COLUMN

There might be a time when you are editing two or three fields only and would like to see the fields side-by-side during the editing process. Access allows you to easily move a column from one location to another within a table by following the steps below:

❶ Click or tap on the title (field name) of the column to be moved. The entire column should become highlighted. To select multiple columns, drag across each column title.

❷ Click or tap on the title <u>again</u> and hold the column's title while dragging the column to its new location.

The mouse pointer will change shape 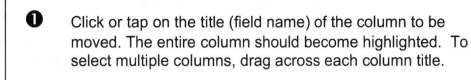 as you begin dragging the column.

You should also notice that as you drag the column left or right, a dark vertical line indicates where the column will be placed.

❸ Drag the column(s) to the new location.

❹ When done, release the mouse button or your finger (if using a touch screen).

HIDING COLUMNS

If a table has too many columns (fields) to fit on the screen, you can hide certain columns that are currently not needed. This feature is also useful for hiding columns that you don't want to print.

To hide a column or group of columns, follow the steps below:

❶

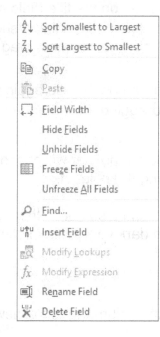

A↓ Z	Sort Smallest to Largest
Z↓ A	Sort Largest to Smallest
🗐	Copy
📋	Paste
↔	Field Width
	Hide Fields
	Unhide Fields
▥	Freeze Fields
	Unfreeze All Fields
🔍	Find...
ᵘ↑ᵘ	Insert Field
🔍	Modify Lookups
ƒx	Modify Expression
▥	Rename Field
✗	Delete Field

To hide a single column (field), point to the column heading (the field name) and click the **[RIGHT]** mouse button or tap and hold (if using a touch screen).

To hide multiple columns, select each column and then click or tap within one of the selected columns (not on any of the column headings) and click the **[RIGHT]** mouse button or tap and hold (if using a touch screen device).

❷ From the pop-up menu, select **Hide Fields**.

The selected column (field) or group of columns will be removed from view, but not removed from the table.

TIP:	*You can also hide a column by changing its size to zero by dragging the column margin to the left.*

UNHIDING COLUMNS

To show a hidden column (field):

❶

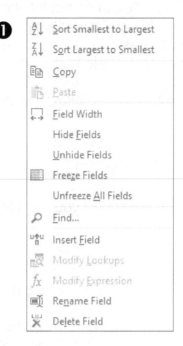

Point to any column (field) heading and then click the **[RIGHT]** mouse button or tap and hold (if using a touch screen device).

From the pop-up menu, choose **Unhide Fields**.

The following dialog box will be displayed:

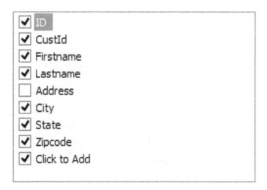

Field names with checkmarks are currently displayed. Those without a checkmark are hidden columns. Check each of the fields you want to unhide. You can also use this box to hide columns by removing the checkmark of the column(s) to hide. As you mark/unmark the columns, you will see them displayed/hidden in the table (behind the dialog box).

When done, click or tap on ⬚ Close ⬚.

FREEZING COLUMNS

If you have a really wide table and find that as you scroll to the right, the columns (fields) on the left side disappear, you can "freeze" some of the columns along the left. By "freezing" these columns, you can easily scroll to the right and still see the company names (as an example) along the left.

To freeze a column (field), follow the steps outlined below:

❶   Arrange the columns in the order you want to have them along the left edge (through moving and hiding).

❷   Select the column(s) you want to freeze.

❸

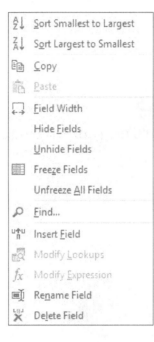

A↓Z	Sort Smallest to Largest
Z↓A	Sort Largest to Smallest
🖹	Copy
🖺	Paste
↔	Field Width
	Hide Fields
	Unhide Fields
▦	Freeze Fields
	Unfreeze All Fields
🔍	Find...
ᵘ↑ᵘ	Insert Field
	Modify Lookups
fx	Modify Expression
🖼	Rename Field
✗	Delete Field

Click the **[RIGHT]** mouse button or tap and hold (if using a touch screen device).

From the pop-up menu, choose **Freeze Fields**.

Once frozen, when you scroll to the right the selected columns will stay on the left edge of the screen.

UNFREEZING COLUMNS

If you no longer need columns (fields) to be frozen, you can choose to "unfreeze" them so that all of the columns will scroll again, as shown below:

Point to the column (field) heading area and click the **[RIGHT]** mouse button or tap and hold (if using a touch screen).

From the pop-up menu, choose **Unfreeze All Fields**.

You cannot unfreeze just a few columns. You must unfreeze all the columns and then freeze the one or two columns you want frozen again.

Instructor Note:

This section is fun for students so allow plenty of time for them to play around.

Instructor Note:

Let students play around with various fonts.

CHANGING THE APPEARANCE OF TEXT

The appearance of the text within fields can be adjusted in a variety of ways. Access allows you to change the typeface, size and style of the datasheet text.

ASSIGNING A NEW FONT

You can emphasize text by changing its font. Make sure the table is visible and is the active tab before continuing.

❶ Click or tap on the down arrow ▾ to the right of the **Font** tool (within the **Text Formatting** section of the Home Ribbon).

❷ Select the desired font from the pull-down list.

CHANGING THE POINT SIZE

❶ Click or tap on the down arrow ▾ beside the **Font Size** tool (from the **Text Formatting** section of the Home Ribbon).

❷ Select the desired font size from the pull-down list.

TURNING ATTRIBUTES ON/OFF

To apply an attribute, click on one of the tools shown below (all of which are located within the **Text Formatting** section of the Home Ribbon). Unless you are in a long text field, these attribute settings will affect the display of the entire table. Long text fields can have a "rich text" setting that allows that single field to have different attributes than the rest of the table.

B   Click or tap this tool to turn **bold** on and off.

I   Click or tap this tool to turn *italics* on and off.

<u>U</u>   Click or tap this tool to turn <u>underline</u> on and off.

A ▾   Click or tap on this tool to change the font color.

ab ▾   Use this tool to highlight a block of text (within a large text field that has been formatted to use "rich text").

▾   Click or tap this tool to apply a background color.

TURNING HIGHLIGHT ON/OFF

When working on a database with someone else, you may want to highlight text so that it stands out - just as you would with a yellow highlighter pen.

This item is only available in long text fields that have been formatted to use "rich text."

To highlight a selected block of text, follow these steps:

❶   Select the text that you want highlighted.

❷   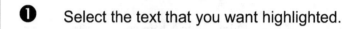 Click or tap on this tool to use the last selected highlight color or click on the down arrow ⏷ beside the **Text Highlight Color** tool (located within the **Text Formatting** section on the Home Ribbon) to choose another color.

❸   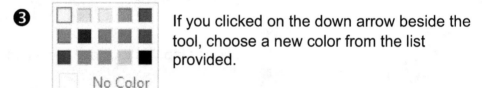 If you clicked on the down arrow beside the tool, choose a new color from the list provided.

CHANGING THE COLOR OF THE FONT

Although Access defaults to printing your text in black, if you have a color printer you can change the color of the font by accessing the Home Ribbon, as shown in the steps below:

❶ Click or tap on this tool to use the last selected color or click on the down arrow ⊡ beside the **Font Color** tool (located within the **Formatting Text** section on the Home Ribbon) to choose another font color.

❷ Select the color you want to use (from the pull-down list) for the selected text.

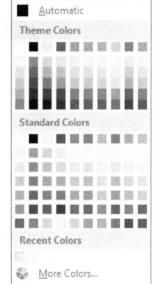

❸ The new font color will be applied to the selected text. Otherwise, the new font color begins at the current cursor location and continues until the end of the field or until you change it again.

> **NOTE:**   *The color you chose last becomes the default. If you look at the tool, the current color will be shown (as an underline for the letter A on the tool).*

Instructor Note:

Remind students that they have to have a color printer to take advantage of these options.

To view the complete color palette, click or tap 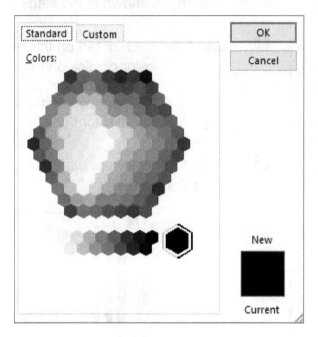 More Colors...

The following dialog box will be displayed:

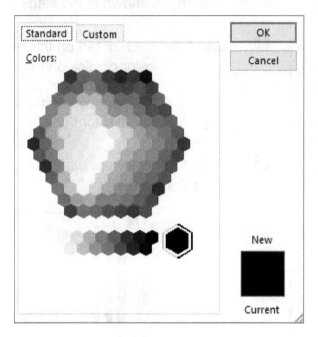

The first tab (labeled **Standard**) allows you to select from a group of predefined colors.

The box in the lower right corner of the dialog box will display the current font color as well as the new color you select.

The second color tab (labeled **Custom**) allows you to further customize the color applied to the text, as shown below:

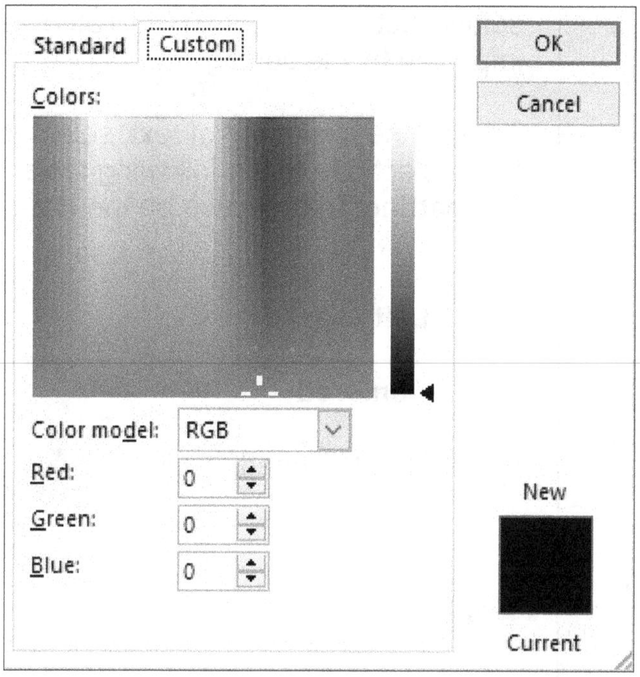

Unless you know the exact values for a particular color, follow the steps shown below to choose a custom color:

❶   Click or tap in the palette area on the color to customize. Notice the bottom right corner of the screen contains a box labeled **Current**. Be sure you see the color to customize in that box before continuing to the second step.

❷   Drag the color marker ◀ up or down to intensify the color. Notice the **New** color box at the bottom of the dialog box.

❸   Once you have the desired color, click or tap OK to close the dialog box.

CHANGING JUSTIFICATION

Access is capable of aligning text to the left, center or right. When setting justification within the Table view, the entire column (field) is impacted by the setting.

To alter the alignment of text, select the text to be modified and then select one of the following tools (located within the **Formatting Text** section on the Home Ribbon):

 **Left** Aligned

Centered

 **Right** Aligned

INDENTING PARAGRAPHS

You can also indent a paragraph within a Rich Text field - which temporarily changes its margins.

Place your cursor in the paragraph to modify and click or tap on one of these tools (located within the **Formatting Text** section on the Home Ribbon) to increase/decrease the indent:

Use these tools to indent/outdent

TEXT DIRECTION

 To specify how text is entered (left-to-right or right-to-left) within a Rich Text field cell, select this tool (located within the **Formatting Text** section on the Home Ribbon).

TURNING BULLETS ON

 To include a bullet list within a Rich Text field, select the **Bullet** tool (located within the **Formatting Text** section on the Home Ribbon).

A bullet will precede each new line.

Select the bullet tool a second time to turn bullets off.

CREATING A NUMBERED LIST

To include a numbered list within a Rich text field, select the **Numbering** tool (located within the **Formatting Text** section on the Home Ribbon).

A number will precede each new line.

Select the tool a second time to turn numbers off.

CHANGING ROW HEIGHT

If the columns are too narrow to display an entire field, you can widen the column (shown previously). However, if you don't want to widen the column(s) you can, instead, choose to increase the row height which will cause the data to wrap to additional lines. The initial row height is set to fit the height of the current font.

If a field doesn't fit within the displayed column width, it is simply truncated (cut-off) to the edge of the column. You don't actually lose any data; you just can't see it until you widen the column. However, if you increase the height of the row to fit two lines of text, any extra data wraps to the next line similar to a paragraph.

To change the row height, follow the steps outlined below:

❶ Position the mouse pointer on the bottom margin line (all the way to the left) of any row. The pointer changes to a black up/down arrow, as illustrated below:

	Customer Id:	Firstname:	Lastname:
Drag the row separator →	100	WILLY	CRUZ
	101	PATRICE	QUEEN
	102	NORA	PULASKI
	103	ALAN	FOXX

❷ Click and hold the **[LEFT]** mouse button while dragging the separator line up or down to increase/decrease the row height as needed.

❸ Once you have the height you want, let go of the mouse. All rows of the datasheet will change to the new row height.

Instructor Note:

Explain that these tools help to format large tables for easier readability.

FORMATTING THE DATASHEET

Use these two tools (located within the Text Formatting section of the Home Ribbon) to define gridlines:

 From the pull-down list, choose which gridlines (vertical, horizontal, neither, or both) to display.

From the pull-down list, select a color to be used as the fill/background color.

For more advanced settings, click or tap on the **Text Formatting Dialog Box Launcher** (located on the Home Ribbon).

Cell Effect	Select what effect to apply to the cells (flat, raised or sunken).
Gridlines Shown	Check whether you would like to have **horizontal** and/or **vertical** gridlines.
Background Color	Select the background (cell) color.
Alternate Background Color	Select the background color to be used for alternating rows.
Gridline Color	Select the color for the gridlines.
Border and Line Styles	Sets the border and line style.
Direction	Set the display direction for new objects.

When done, choose OK .

PRACTICE EXERCISE

Instructions:	❶	Open the **Clients** table in datasheet view.
	❷	Open the **Orders** table in datasheet view.
	❸	Adjust the column sizes within the **Clients** table so that all data is visible. Adjust the size of the **Orders** table so that the columns take up as little space as possible without hiding data.
	❹	Change the row height for the **Clients** table so that the address wraps to a second line. You will need to shrink the Address column.
	❺	Move the **ItemCode** field to the second column within the **Orders** view.
	❻	Clear both tables from view (saving your settings) and then view the **Orders** table again to ensure the settings have been saved.

SORTING THE DATA

USAGE:

Instructor Note:

Show students how easy it is to sort a table.

As you work with your data, you may find that the records are not in any particular order. As a result, reading or finding a specific record may be difficult, especially if you have hundreds or thousands of records. Access has an easy way of rearranging/sorting data so that you can print/view the records in the order needed.

Before you sort, click or tap anywhere in the field you want to sort. For example, if you want to sort alphabetically by last names, make sure your cursor is somewhere in that field.

Once you have selected the field on which to sort, select one of the following tools (located within the **Sort & Filter** section of the Home Ribbon):

A↓ Ascending   Click or tap this tool to sort the records in ascending (alphabetical/lowest to highest) sequence.

Z↓ Descending   Click or tap this tool to sort the records in descending (reverse-alphabetical/highest to lowest) sequence.

> **NOTE:**   *You can also sort a column by clicking or tapping on the down arrow* ▾ *beside that column/field's name and choosing the sort order you wish to use.*

A Z▸ Remove Sort   Click on this tool to remove the sort and return the list to its original display.

SORTING ON MULTIPLE FIELDS

To sort on more than one field at a time, you must select all the fields (columns) on which to sort by. Access will sort by the leftmost column first followed by each of the other selected fields in order from left to right.

You may need to move the columns around to get them in the order needed. For example, to sort employees by last name and then by first names, you will need to rearrange the columns so that the first name column comes after the last name column.

PRINT PREVIEWING

USAGE:

Although Access has an extensive report generator (discussed later), you may find yourself having to print a quick list of your records without any special formatting features. Before you print your table, you should preview the printout to make sure that it will print to your satisfaction.

Open the **File Ribbon** and choose **Print**.

Select **Print Preview** from the submenu.

Print Preview
Preview and make changes to pages before printing.

The Print Preview screen will be displayed:

The following sections are available within the preview window:

This first section contains the print button for immediately printing the current document.

The second section is used to define the paper size as well as buttons to display/hide the margins and the data.

This section defines page orientation, columns and the page setup.

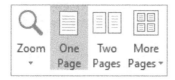

The fourth section is used to change the print preview display. Notice there are tools to set a specific zoom factor as well as tools for choosing to view one page, two pages or more.

When done, click or tap on this button to **Close** the print preview and return to the editing screen.

PAGE SETUP

USAGE:

If you need to change the paper size, page orientation, margins, or other features that affect the page layout, you will need to access the **Page Setup** box, as shown below:

Page Setup

Click or tap this button (within the Print Preview screen).

The following dialog box will be displayed:

CHANGING MARGINS

Be sure that the first tab labeled **Print Options** has been selected at the top of the screen. As mentioned, you can adjust the top, bottom, left or right margins.

A preview box is provided on the right side of this dialog box to see how your new margin settings will change the document. This box also allows you to display/hide headings as well as specify whether only the form or only the datasheet should be printed.

CHANGING PAPER SIZE

To change the paper size and/or page orientation, select the second tab at the top of the screen, labeled **Page**.

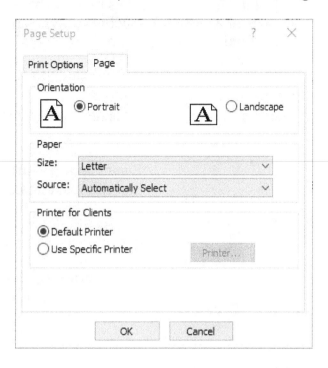

Orientation The page orientation (portrait or landscape) can be changed by clicking on the appropriate radio button.

Paper Click or tap on the down arrow ⌄ to the right of the "Paper Size" section to select from one of many predefined sizes. You may also select the source (tray) for the paper.

Printer Allows you to specify the printer to be used. Click or tap Printer... to choose a printer other than the default.

Once settings have been changed, select OK .

PRINTING THE TABLE

USAGE:

Instructor Note:

Whether the students are connected to a printer or not, be sure to take them into this dialog box and discuss each of the print options.

Although Access has an extensive report generator (discussed in the last module of this manual), you may find yourself needing to print a quick list of your records without any special formatting features. When you print a table within Access, the program defaults to a tabular report, using the table's name as a header along with the current date and page number.

Open the **File Ribbon** and choose **Print**.

Select **Quick Print** to bypass the Print dialog box and accepting the defaults.

Select **Print** if you would like to change printers, print specific records or print more than one copy of the table.

If you selected **Print**, the following dialog box will be displayed:

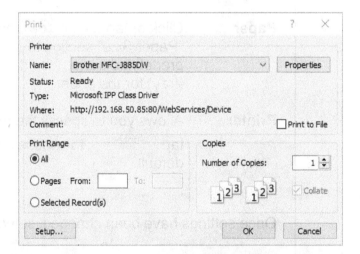

Select the printer, enter the number of copies desired, and select which pages (or records) you want printed.

When done, select OK .

PRACTICE EXERCISE

Instructions:	❶	Open the **Clients** table in datasheet view.
	❷	Sort the records by last name.
	❸	Next, sort the records by city, last name, first name - in that order.
	❹	Print/Preview the listing.

Module Four

- **Creating a Database**
- **Designing a Table**
- **Restructuring a Table**

CREATING A DATABASE

USAGE:

Although you will probably work with existing files most of the time, you will also want to create your own database at some point.

You can choose to create the database from one of the built-in template designs or from one of your own existing files. A template is used to determine the basic structure of the database and contains predefined settings, such as fields.

Instructor Note:

Explain that although the majority of their time will be spent working on existing databases, at some point they will need to know how to create one from scratch.

Instructor Note:

Just like the other Office 365 products (Word, Excel, PowerPoint, Publisher), Access provides a number of templates to make creating a new database easier.

Open the **File Ribbon** and choose **New**.

This window contains a list of available templates for creating web-based applications, standard desktop databases or some common predefined applications.

If you don't see a template matching your requirements, use the search box across the top of the window to try to locate a template that might work or can be easily modified.

Click or tap on the template you wish to use.

If you chose to create a blank database, you'll need to assign a name to it:

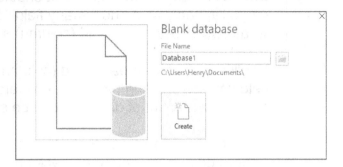

In the box provided, enter the name you would like to assign to the database you are creating.

Click or tap on to search your system for the location you want to use to store the new database.

Once you have selected where you want to store the new database and assigned a name to it, click or tap on this button to actually create it.

This new blank database will function as the container for the tables, forms and other objects that you will use to work with your actual data.

Instructor Note:

Have students design a simple database based on one of the existing templates. Point out the fields that are already included in that database.

Next, have them create a blank database and add their own fields.

Instructor Note:

Show students how to pop back-and-forth between design and database view.

DESIGNING A TABLE

Before creating a new table, you should sit down and plan it out carefully, deciding on how many fields (columns) you need and what type of data each field (column) should store.

You'll need to name each field (column header), specify the type of field you are creating (numeric, text, etc.) and, in some cases, define the amount of data that can be stored in that field.

If you create a table and then decide the design is incorrect, Access does allow you to go back and redesign it but, depending on the redesign, you may lose some of your data. That's why pre-planning is so important.

If you had created a database from one of the available templates, Access would have automatically included a list of fields that would be associated with the type of template you chose.

However, if created a blank database, the table will be empty so you'll need to design it yourself, starting with a blank screen:

Although you can immediately begin entering data, you will probably want to first define the fields/columns and the type of data to be stored in each of those fields/columns. Although you can immediately begin entering data, you will probably want to first define the fields/columns and the type of data to be stored in each of those fields/columns.

If you are defining a simple table and already know the basic layout (field types), you can click or tap on the down arrow beside this column header to select the type of field for that column.

Once you select the type of field, you can change the default field name to a more descriptive one.

If you have a more complicated layout and/or need more control over the type of fields and their format, you will need to switch to the Design View:

 Click or tap on this tool (located in the lower right corner of the status bar) to switch to Design View.

You can also switch to Design View by clicking or tapping on this tool (located on the far left of the Field Ribbon) and choosing from the pull-down list of available views.

Before switching to Design View, you will be asked to save the table and name it:

Table Name:

Table1

OK   Cancel

Enter a name in the box provided and then click or tap OK .

The following screen will be displayed:

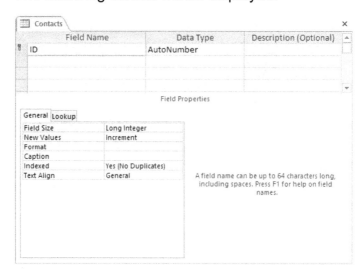

There are three sections within this window. Use the first section to define the name, data type and description for each field within your table:

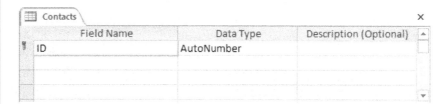

Use the **Field Properties** section to further customize the properties of a particular field.

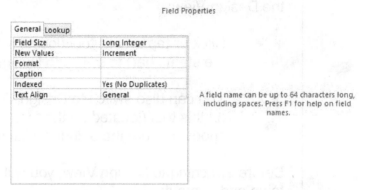

The **Property Sheet** is used to define advanced options for the table data. These properties define advanced characteristics and behavior of tables and fields that should only be changed if you know what you are doing. If you aren't going to be using this section you can click or tap on the **X** in the upper right corner of this section to close it.

FIELD NAMES

When adding/changing fields, you need to provide some basic information about the field, such as the "name" and "type" of data that will be stored in the field. Field names can be up to 64 characters in length and may contain letters, numbers and spaces.

Although you can use up to 64 characters, you should try to keep field names as short as possible since you will be referring to them quite often when creating forms, reports and other objects. However, don't make them too short so they can't be recognized.

FIELD TYPES

Instructor Note:

Go slowly over each of the types of fields available and the rules for each.

Once you have labeled a field with a name, you must identify the "type" of data that will be stored within the field. In the column labeled "Data Type" select the type of data to be stored in that field.

To choose field types other than text, move to the **Data Type** column and click or tap on the down arrow ⌄ to see the list of available types.

Click or tap on the desired field type.

Field Type	Description
Short Text	Stores up to 255 characters of alphanumeric data (names, address, etc.)
Long Text	Stores larger amounts of alphanumeric data.
Number	Stores numerical data for calculations, within a range of -2^{31} to $2^{31}-1$.
Large Number	Used for very large numbers and is compatible with the SQL Server bigint. Stores numerical data for calculations, within a range of -2^{63} to $2^{63}-1$.
Date/Time	Stores dates and times.
Currency	Numbers with dollar signs (up to 4 decimals).
AutoNumber	Assigns a random or sequential number.
Yes/No	Contains only one of two values. Used for true/false, on/off and yes/no entries.
OLE Object	Used for storing objects, such as spreadsheets, pictures or other objects from Windows apps.
Hyperlink	Use this if you want to store links to documents or files stored on the Internet or local network.
Attachment	Use this for attaching documents, spreadsheets, pictures, etc. to the record. You can have an unlimited number of attachments (up to the database storage limit).
Calculated	Uses one or more data fields to formulate a calculation and stores the results in this field.
Lookup Wizard	Looks up values in another table or combo box.

FIELD DESCRIPTIONS

Since you will normally keep your field names to a minimum size, you might want to use this section to further clarify the contents of the field. Remember that this description is displayed on the status line whenever the user enters this field. The description can be used to explain the field in more detail or to give special instructions.

INSERTING A FIELD

There may be times when you decide that a new field should be placed between two existing ones. To insert the field, move to the location where the new field should appear.

Insert Rows — Click or tap on this button (within the **Tools** section on the Design Ribbon) to insert a blank row (field).

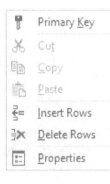

You can also click the **[RIGHT]** mouse button or tap and hold (if using a touch screen) and choose **Insert Rows** from the pop-up menu. The current row is pushed down and a blank row appears for you to enter the contents of the new field.

DELETING A FIELD

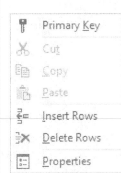

Delete Rows   Click or tap on this button (located within the **Tools** section on the Design Ribbon) to delete the current row (field).

You can also point to the row containing the field you want to remove and click the **[RIGHT]** mouse button or tap and hold (if suing a touch screen device). Choose **Delete Rows** from the pop-up menu.

NOTE:	If the database contains information, you'll be asked to confirm the deletion.

CHANGING FIELD SIZE

If you find that a field is too small or too long, you can adjust the size to a more appropriate one. The field size is set in the lower half of the design screen where the field **properties** are.

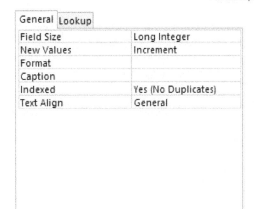

Instructor Note:

Go over each of the rules with the students.

Small Text fields can be a maximum of 255 characters in length. **Numeric** fields have several different size limitations depending on the size of the number you plan to store. You can choose from byte, integer, long integer, single, double, replication ID and decimal.

Field Size	Numeric Size
Byte	Stores numbers from 0 to 255. No decimals.
Integer	From -32,768 to 32,767 without decimals.
Long Integer	Stores numbers from -2,147,483,648 to 2,147,483,647. No decimals allowed.
Single	Numbers from -3.4x1038 to 3.4x1038 with up to 7 decimal places.
Double	From -1.797x10308 to 1.797x10308 with up to 15 decimal places.
Replication ID	A unique ID used for replication purposes.
Decimal	Stores numbers up to 28 decimal places.

TIP:	*Select the smallest number possible. Access works faster and more efficiently with smaller values.*

VIEWING THE CHANGES

When done modifying the table design, click or tap on ⊞ (located in the right corner of the status bar) which switches to the datasheet view. Since you cannot add/view records until the changes are saved, the following box appears:

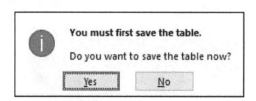

You must first save the table.

Do you want to save the table now?

[Yes]   [No]

Click or tap [Yes] to save your changes.

Instructor Note:

Have students now add a few records to their new table.

ADDING RECORDS TO THE TABLE

Once you have designed the table, you will be ready to begin adding records.

Be sure you have switched back to the datasheet view.

Notice that the table is set up similar to an Excel spreadsheet whereby the field names are labeled across the top of each column and the records are stored in the rows underneath.

You may now simply begin typing in the information for each record. Press [TAB] or [ENTER] to move from field to field.

When you reach the end of a record, pressing [TAB] or [ENTER] will move you to the next record.

If you make a mistake while typing, use the [←BACKSPACE] or [DEL] key to correct the error.

DELETING A RECORD

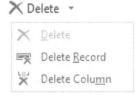

If you have entered a record and now wish to remove it, click or tap on this button (located within the **Records** section on the Home Ribbon) and select "Delete Record" from the pull-down list.

You will need to confirm the deletion of the record:

Click or tap [Yes] to confirm the deletion.

RENAMING A DATABASE OBJECT

If you decide to change the name of a table (or any other database object), you can easily do so from within the database window.

To do so, follow the steps outlined below:

❶   Select the table's icon (or the icon representing the object you want to rename).

❷   Click or tap on the object's name - to select it.

❸   Press F2.

❹   The current name of the object will be selected. Begin editing or changing the name, as needed.

❺   When done, click/tap away or press ENTER.

Instructor Note:

Point out the bottom note since students often click twice too quickly and open the object by mistake.

NOTE:	Be sure to close the object (e.g., table or form) to be renamed before following the steps above.

PRACTICE EXERCISE

Instructions: ❶ Create a new table.

❷ Add the following fields to your new table:

Field Name
ProductID
ProductName
UnitPrice

❸ Name the new table **Items.**

❹ Add the following records to the table:

ProductID	ProductName	UnitPrice
1	Chia Pet	12
2	Pet Rock	10
3	Ginsu Knife Set	22
4	PEZ Dispenser	5
5	Lava Lamp	13.65

❺ Print/Preview the record listing for the **Items** table.

REDESIGNING A TABLE

USAGE:

Instructor Note:

Emphasize that at some point they will need to redesign an existing table (forgot a field that needed to be included or added a field that is not needed).

The most often instance is designating the wrong field type when creating the table.

It is unrealistic to believe you will never make a mistake when creating tables. At some point you will probably need to go back and alter the design of an existing table. After having worked with the table, you may realize that you missed a field, made a field too short, or come across some other problem.

Although good planning can help avoid many of these problems, real life situations almost always point out deficiencies in our designs. The good news is that you can easily redesign and customize your tables even after data has been entered.

To modify a table's design, click or tap on ✍ (located in the lower right corner of the status bar).

Field Properties

General	Lookup	
Field Size	Long Integer
New Values	Increment
Format	
Caption	
Indexed	Yes (No Duplicates)
Text Align	General

A field name can be up to 64 characters long, including spaces. Press F1 for help on field names.

The top section of the window will be used to identify the name, type of data and an optional description for each field.

> **NOTE:** The field description can be used to display more information on the status line. For example, you could display instructions for filling out the field info.

THE TABLE DESIGN TOOLS

While in design mode, the Table Tools Design Ribbon is automatically selected and the following tools are available:

View

Use this tool to switch back to datasheet view.

Primary Key

Sets current field as the primary key. A primary key is used to uniquely identify each record for storage purposes. Typically, a field containing non-repeating data (such as a social security number of Employee ID) is used as the primary key within a database.

Builder

Click or tap this tool to access the Field Builder which allows you to add fields from a list of categories.

Test Validation Rules

Use this tool to test validation rules that you may have set for a field within your database. For example, you may have set a rule for zip codes to ensure that only numbers are entered.

 Insert Rows

Inserts a blank row for a new field to be added at the current location.

 Delete Rows

Deletes the current row/field.

 Modify Lookups

Click or tap this tool to create a special field containing related data from another table. This field is displayed as a pull-down list from which you can choose a value. For example, instead of having to type in a state, you can create a lookup column containing a list of states from which to choose.

Property Sheet

Displays a list of advanced settings for the table or individual fields.

Indexes

Use this tool to create indexes for other fields that are searched or sorted on a regular basis. Indexing speeds up the process of searching and sorting.

PRACTICE EXERCISE

Instructions:

❶ Open the **Items** table in design mode and change the length of the **ProductName** field to 15.

❷ Add the following fields to the table:

Field Name	Type	Field Size
SellPrice	Currency	
OnhandQty	Number	Integer

❸ Add the following data to the records:

ProductID	ProductName	SellPrice	OnhandQty
1	Chia Pet	35.00	257
2	Pet Rock	27.50	1247
3	Ginsu Knife Set	63.95	329
4	Pez Dispenser	8.95	3471
5	Lava Lamp	13.65	87

❹ Open the **Clients** in design mode and make the following changes:

FieldName	Field Size
CustID	Byte
Firstname	20
Lastname	20
Address	30
City	20
State	2
Zipcode	5

❺ Open the **Orders** in design mode and make the following changes:

FieldName	Field Type	Field Size
CustID		Byte
ItemCode		Byte
Quantity		Integer
SaleAmount	Currency	

Module Five

- **Filtering Records**
- **Finding Data**

FILTERING RECORDS

USAGE:

Since a table can be quite large, there may be times when you need to display records based on specific conditions. Asking Access to list a specific group of records is called **filtering**. After you create a filter, the program hides all the records that do not match your filter criteria. Although you can use simple filters, you can also use the filter to create more complex sorting options.

The simplest way to filter data is to click or tap the down arrow ⌄ beside the column you want to use to filter your records.

From the pull-down list, uncheck the box marked (**Select All**) and then check the box of the item you want to use to filter.

When done, click or tap ⸢ OK ⸥.

Instructor Note:

This section will take a bit longer so plan on beginning it after a break when students are fresh.

Begin by discussing why you'd want to filter your table and then begin the actual process.

For example, to view only those records containing addresses in California, you would click on the down arrow ⌄ beside the field storing states, uncheck the box marked (Select All), and then check the box beside "CA", and click or tap ⸢ OK ⸥.

If you wanted to view the records containing addresses within a specific city within California, you would first click or tap on the down arrow ⌄ beside the field containing states and make sure that only the box for "CA" was checked. You would then move to the field containing cities to ensure that only the city you wanted to filter by was checked.

The down arrow ⌄ beside the field being filtered will display a small filter icon, indicating that the records are being filtered based on that field.

Filter

To quickly access the filter pull-down, move to the field you wish to use as your filter and click or tap this button (within the **Sort & Filter** section on the Home Ribbon) or click/tap on the down arrow ⌄ beside the column heading.

VIEWING ALL RECORDS

Once you choose to filter the database to display only specific records, you can quickly switch back to viewing all of the records by clicking on the down arrow ⬇ beside the column(s) you have filtered and then marking the (Select All) box.

USING THE SELECTION FILTER

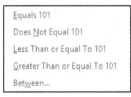

To quickly filter by the currently selected entry, click or tap this button (within the **Sort & Filter** section on the Home Ribbon).

From the pull-down list, you will be able to filter your records to include only those records that equal, don't equal, contains, or don't contain the currently selected data.

CREATING TEXT AND NUMBER FILTERS

While the AutoFilter makes it easy to select records based on a specific entry in your table, there may be times when you will want to display rows of data that meet different criteria. For example, you may want to list all records that have a city name beginning with the letter 'A' which would include Anaheim and Aliso Viejo.

Click or tap on the down arrow ⬇ beside the field you want to create a text filter for and then select **Text Filters** or **Number Filters** from the drop-down list.

A box will be provided to enter the criteria you are searching for based on the argument (equals, does not equal, etc.) you chose.

USING THE FORM FILTER

This feature displays a form from which you can select the data that you want to display based on more advanced criteria. Follow the steps outlined below:

❶    Click or tap this tool (located within the Sort & Filter section on the Home Ribbon).

❷    From the pull-down list, select **Filter by Form**. The datasheet view will be replaced with one row similar to the one shown below:

Code	Parkname	Address1	Address2	City	State

❸ Select the field containing the data you want to search for. A small pull-down arrow ⬇ will appear.

❹ Click or tap the down arrow ⬇. A list of unique values for that field will be displayed. Simply select the data that represents the rows to be displayed.

If you want to be more precise, you can select more fields of data which will narrow the records. For example, you could select a state and then a city within the state.

To search for more than one group of records, there is a set of tabs located at the bottom of the filter, as shown below:

Click or tap the first **Or** tab to select another set of criteria to filter. The rows matching this set of criteria will be displayed **in addition** to those that match your first tab (or any additional **Or** tabs). For example, you might want to search for more than one city at a time.

❺ ▼ Toggle Filter

Once you have defined all your criteria for the filter, click or tap on this tool to actually apply the filter and display the records that match your selected data.

▼ Filtered

Notice the bottom of the datasheet just to the right of the record counter contains this new button. Click or tap it to toggle back and forth between the filtered and unfiltered data.

> **NOTE:** Whenever a data table is filtered, you will see the word **Filtered** displayed along the right side of the status bar.

PERFORMING QUICK SEARCHES

Search

Notice the bottom of the datasheet just to the right of the Filtered/Unfiltered button is another new section labeled "Search".

Click or tap in this box to enter data you wish to quickly search for.

As soon as you begin typing, Access will move to the datasheet to highlight the first record meeting the search criteria entered.

WORKING WITH ADVANCED FILTERS

To create an advanced filter, you should be viewing the table that is to be filtered. You can be in the datasheet or the form view.

❶

Click or tap this tool (located within the **Sort & Filter** section on the Home Ribbon).

❷

From the pull-down menu, select **Advanced Filter/Sort...**

The following window will be displayed:

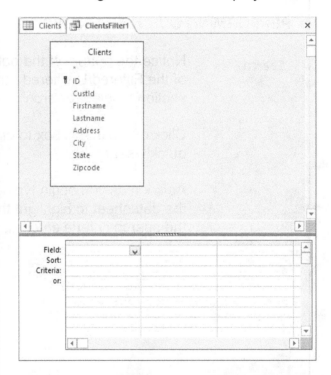

Access will display all of the fields within the selected table but none of the actual data will be seen.

The bottom section is where you will specify your filter criteria.

The following sections are shown in the bottom part of the screen:

Field   Use this section to enter the name of the field that you want to query.

Sort   Click or tap here to sort on this field in ascending or descending order. You can also use this section to remove sorting.

Criteria   This is where you actually type in what you are searching for. Be sure to place your criteria in the column of the field that contains the data you are searching for.

Or   If you are looking for more than one item within the same column (field), you can place your criteria on multiple lines.

❸   To add a field, click or tap in the box labeled "Field" and choose from the pull-down list. You can also drag the field from the table (in the top section) into this section.

❹   **ENTERING CRITERIA**

Once you have added the fields to be searched, your next step is to tell Access what your condition is. Move to the field where the condition is to be set and enter the criteria. The following operators may be used for a filter:

$$= \quad > \quad < \quad >= \quad <=$$

If you were searching for those employees making more than $40,000.00 you would move to the salary field and enter:

>40000

If you want more than one condition to be met, you may enter conditions in more than one field on the <u>same row</u>. This tells Access that all conditions must be met in order for the records to be listed.

If you want to look for a range of values within the same field, use the **And** operator. For example, to display those employees who make between $30,000 and $40,000 per year, you would move to the salary field and enter:

>=30000 AND <=40000

In the scenario mentioned above, only records where employees made at least $30,000 and no more than $40,000 would be listed.

If, instead, you want one or the other condition to be met within the same field the word **OR** is used. For example, to find those employees who work in the Admin or Accounting departments you would move to the department field and enter:

Admin or Accounting

The **OR** tells Access that just one of the two conditions must be met in order for the records to be displayed.

If you want to display records based on an OR existing between <u>different</u> fields, you must use two lines during the querying process. For example, if you are searching for employees working in the Admin department <u>or</u> those employees making more than $30,000 regardless of their department you would first move to the salary field and enter:

>30000

And then you would move down to the next criteria row and over to the department field and enter:

Admin

If both conditions are on the same row, Access assumes you want both conditions to be met. In other words, this is considered an **AND** statement whereas two separate lines are considered an **OR** statement. You can be as selective as you want by using several lines to include several **OR** conditions.

Access provides a method by which you can search for a "pattern" of characters using the asterisk (*) as a "wildcard" symbol.

This is especially useful when you are unsure how to spell a name.

Examples include the following:

Instructor Note:

Be sure to include wildcard searches.

This pattern...	...would find these:
S*	Smith, sugar
g*t	Giant, gross weight
*D	Grand, Elm Road
*e*s	Phillip Edward Wilson, roses
7*5	7485, 70,005
10/*/18	All dates in October 2018

In addition to the asterisk, there are a few other wildcard characters that can be used during a filter, as described below:

Symbol	Example	Description
?	b?ll	Matches any single character. (Finds ball, bell, and bill)
#	1#3	Matches a single digit. (Finds 103, 113, 123)
[ ]	b[ui]ll	Matches any single character within the brackets. (Finds bill, bull not ball)
!	b[!ui]ll	Matches any character not in list. (Finds bell, ball not bull)
-	b[a-c]d	Matches any one of a range of characters. (Finds bad, bbd, and bcd)

❺  Toggle Filter   Click or tap on this tool to apply the filter to your table.

If you need to make a change to the filter, you can access the **Advanced Filter** option again.

> **NOTE:**   *If you want to keep this filter for future use, you must save the filter as a query from within a filter form or advanced filter view.*

Instructor Note:

It's very important that students know how to remove a filter once it's been created.

REMOVING A FILTER

After you have used a filter, you may want to return to viewing all of the records in the table again.

Toggle Filter   Click or tap on this tool to show all of your records again.

PRACTICE EXERCISE

Instructions:	❶	Make sure you are viewing the **Clients** table.
	❷	Create a filter that will find all the clients living in "Los Angeles".
	❸	Change the filter to list all records from the state of Tennessee as well as Kansas. Sort the records by last name.
	❹	Print/Preview the listing.
	❺	Clear the filter so that all records are once again displayed.

FINDING DATA

USAGE:

Access has a handy feature that works like a search/find option in a word processor. You simply enter the text/data you are looking for and Access can search the current column or all columns for a match. You can be in any field column when you want to find something, but if you plan on searching within just one field, you should make sure your cursor is somewhere in the field column you will be searching. This will speed up the search.

Follow the steps outlined below to find data:

❶ Click or tap this tool (within the **Find** section on the Home Ribbon) and select the tab labeled **Find**.

Find

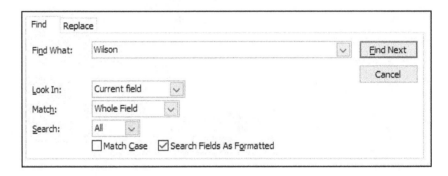

> **Instructor Note:**
>
> *This subject is quite simple so should go quickly.*
>
> *Point out that it's the same as in the other Office products.*

❷ Use the **Find What** text box to enter the text/data to find. Click or tap the down arrow ⌄ beside the **Look In** section to select the field to use for the search.

(OPTIONAL)

❸ In the section labeled **Match**, define whether the text must match just part of a field, that the whole field must match, or that the text must be found at the start/beginning of a field.

(OPTIONAL)

❹ Click or tap the down arrow ⌄ beside the **Search** box to select the direction in which the search should proceed. Choose "Up" to search from the current position to the beginning of the table or "Down" to search to the end of the table. Select "All" to search all records - regardless of which record you are currently viewing.

(OPTIONAL)

❺ Check the box labeled **Match Case** to ensure all upper and lowercase characters match exactly as you entered them.

(OPTIONAL)

❻ **Search fields as formatted** should be checked to search a field exactly the way it is displayed in the table. For example, a date is stored as 10/1/18 but may be displayed as 01-Oct-18.

❼ Once you have made your selections, click or tap [Find Next] to find the first and additional occurrences of the text.

You can also search for a "pattern" of characters using the asterisk (*) as a "wildcard" symbol.

Examples include the following:

This pattern...	...would find these:
S*	Smith, sugar
g*t	Giant, gross weight
*D	Grand, Elm Road
7*5	7485, 735
10/*/18	All dates in October of 2018

There are a few other wildcard characters, as described below:

Symbol	Example	Description
?	b?ll finds ball and , bell, and bill	Matches any single character.
#	1#3 finds 103, 113, 123	Matches a single digit.
[ ]	b[ui]ll finds bill, bull not ball	Matches any single character within the brackets.
!	b[!ui]ll finds bell, ball not bull	Matches any character not in list.
-	b[a-c]d finds bad, bbd, and bcd	Matches any of a range of characters.

PRACTICE EXERCISE

Instructions:	❶	Make sure you are viewing the **Clients** table.
	❷	Using the "find" option, find anyone living on "Gall" street.
	❸	Find all the records with a last name of "Wilson".

Module Six

- **Creating Reports**

CREATING REPORTS

USAGE:

Instructor Note:

The last module deals with creating basic reports.

Since reports are also covered in both the intermediate and advanced classes, it's not necessary to go into too much detail here.

Access allows you to quickly create basic reports with the use of a single tool on the ribbon. You can also design more detailed, custom reports using the Report Wizard which steps you through the process of designing the report.

Click or tap this tool (within the **Reports** section on the Create Ribbon) to have Access create a basic report based on the data in the currently selected table or query.

You will not be prompted to enter any information. Instead, Access will simply create a new tab containing a generic report consisting of the information within the currently selected table or query.

The Design Ribbon will automatically be selected so that you can customize the report if needed. Switch to the Format Ribbon to customize the report.

Click or tap the down arrow ⊡ beside this tool to choose a different font for the selected item.

Click or tap the down arrow ⊡ beside this tool to select a new font size.

Use this tool to turn **bold** on and off.

Click or tap this tool to turn *italics* on and off.

Use this tool to turn <u>underline</u> on and off.

Use this tool to change the font color.

Use this tool to left-align text within the report.

Use this tool to center text.

Click or tap on this tool to right-align text.

This tool is used to copy a format from one area within the report to another. Begin by selecting the text you want to copy the format from and then choose this tool. Your mouse pointer will change shape. You can now "paint" that format onto other report text.

Click or tap this tool to apply a background color.

Alternate Row Color ▾

Alternates the fill/background colors for rows (records).

Conditional Formatting

Click or tap this tool to specify formatting options based on a condition (rule) that you set. For example, you might set the condition (rule) that records containing values between 100 and 200 should be displayed in red.

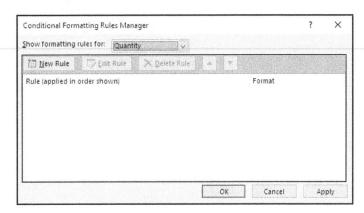

From within the Conditional Formatting dialog box (shown above) select the format to be applied and then the condition that must be met before the format is applied. When done, click or tap [OK]

Number

You can format numeric fields on the report by using these tools on the Format Ribbon.

Click or tap the down arrow ▼ beside this tool to choose from a list of formats.

$ This tool formats the current selection for **currency**.

%   Formats the current selection for **percentage**.

,   Formats the selection for **comma** by adding a comma as a thousand separator and two decimal places.

Increases the number of decimal places displayed.

Decreases the number of decimal places displayed.

Background Image ▾

Use this tool to add a background image to the report.

Themes ▾

From the **Design Ribbon**, choose this tool to quickly apply a theme to your report.

Themes are used to enhance reports, making them appear more professional with the application of uniform color designs.

Notice as you scroll the list. Your report reflects the currently selected theme.

From the pull-down list, select the theme you would like applied to your report.

You can also adjust the width of any column. First, click within the heading of the column you wish to adjust. Next, move the mouse pointer to the right margin of the column heading. The pointer changes to a double-arrow ↔.

Once you see the double-arrow, double-click to automatically adjust the column to accommodate the widest entry, or click and drag to manually adjust the column width.

USING THE REPORT WIZARD

If you want a different style report, you can use the Report Wizard to guide you through the creation process.

 Report Wizard   To access the Report Wizard, select this tool (located within the **Reports** section on the Create Ribbon).

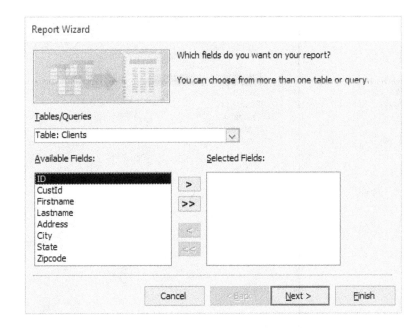

If the table or query name that you want to create the report from is not already displayed in the text box, click or tap on the down arrow ▼ located to the right of this box and select the table/query to use.

Access displays the available fields in the left column and the fields currently selected for your report in the right column.

To add all the fields to your new report, click or tap [>>].

If you only want some of the fields, highlight each field and click or tap on [>] to add one field at a time.

If you accidentally added a wrong field, or decide to remove fields from your new report, use [<<] to remove all the fields, or use [<] to remove one field at a time.

When you are ready to continue, click or tap on [Next >].

The next screen is used to break your report down into groups or categories of records. This is useful for large groups of data and can make your report easier to read. For example, a list of customers could be broken down by state and then by city. The state would be the first group and then cities would be sub-groups under each state.

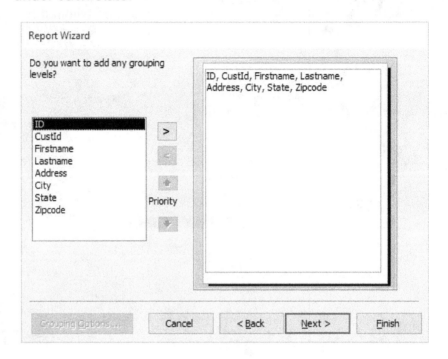

Use the left column of fields to choose what groups of records should be created. For example, you might want the records grouped by state. As you add a field for grouping, you will see the sample on the right adjust to show how the records will be displayed.

If you add more than one field for grouping, you can use the **Priority** arrows to rearrange the order in which the records will be grouped. For example, you might want to group the records first by state and then group by zipcode within each state.

Most users will not need to make additional changes, but if you only want the groups to be determined by the first few characters of a field, access Grouping Options ... and select the number of initial characters to scan before determining its group.

Once you are ready to continue, click or tap Next > .

Next you will be prompted to specify how the report will be sorted, as shown in the diagram below:

```
Report Wizard

What sort order do you want for your records?

                                    You can sort records by up to four fields, in either
                                    ascending or descending order.

                              1   City                    ▼      Ascending

                              2                           ▼      Ascending

                              3                           ▼      Ascending

                              4                           ▼      Ascending


                    Cancel      < Back      Next >      Finish
```

You can select up to four fields on which to sort your data. Use the pull-down arrows ▼ to define which fields to sort the records on and in what order to sort them.

   Click or tap on this button next to each field to define whether that field should be sorted in ascending or descending sequence.

If you selected a field to group in the previous step, Access will automatically sort by that field first. Grouping will also provide the option of summarizing numeric fields for each group. For example, you may want to include a Total Sales amount for each group.

When you are ready to continue, click or tap Next > .

Now you can choose the layout of the report, as shown below:

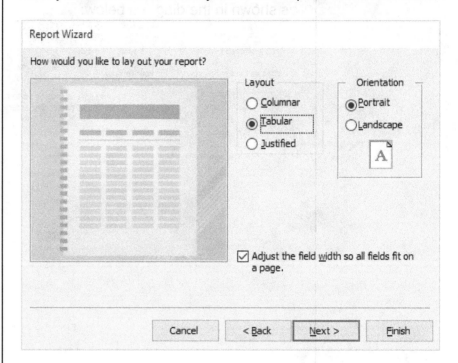

As you make a selection from the **Layout** column, you will see an example of the layout in the left window. This will help you decide which layout best fits your report.

The layout options will be different if you chose to group the records.

You can also change the page **Orientation** to match the type of report you want. Landscape is good if you are trying to fit a lot of columns across one page. Portrait is useful if you don't have many columns but want to fit as many records as you can on a page.

Use the checkbox at the bottom to automatically adjust the field lengths so that all your fields fit on the page. However, if you select this option, some of the fields may be truncated in order to make room for the others.

When you have made a choice, click or tap Next > .

The final step is to name the report, as shown below:

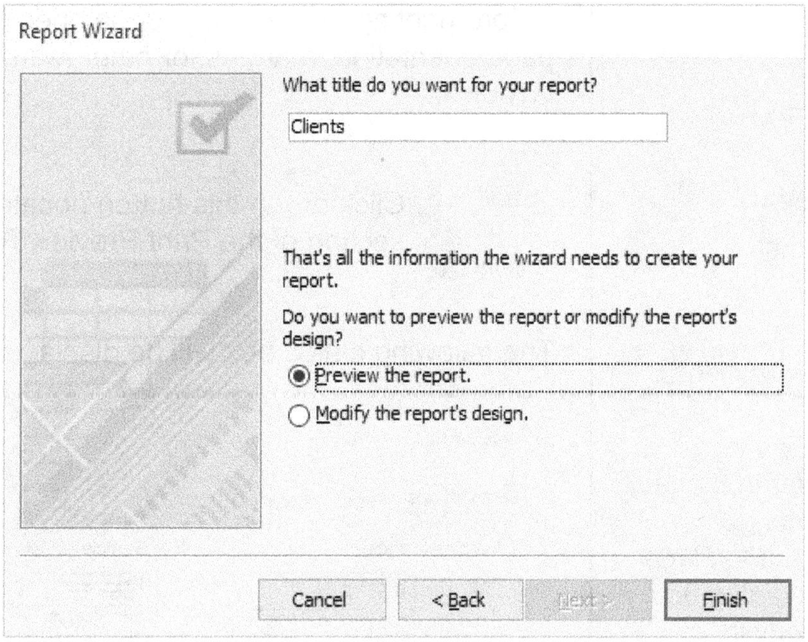

Use the text box at the top to enter a title for your report.

Once the report is done, choose whether you want to **Preview** the final report or to switch to the design mode and **Modify** it.

When you are done, click or tap   Finish   .

Access will now create the report and display the results.

PRINTING OPTIONS

Before printing the report, you may need to change the paper size, page orientation, margins, or other features that affect the page layout.

Page Setup

Click or tap this button (located within the **Page Layout** section of the Print Preview Ribbon).

The following dialog box will be displayed:

CHANGING MARGINS

Be sure that the first tab labeled **Print Options** has been selected at the top of the screen. As mentioned, you can adjust the top, bottom, left or right margins.

A preview box is provided on the right side of this dialog box to see how your new margin settings will change the document. This box also allows you to display/hide headings as well as specify whether only the form or only the datasheet should be printed.

CHANGING PAPER SIZE

To change the paper size and/or page orientation, select the second tab at the top of the screen, labeled **Page**.

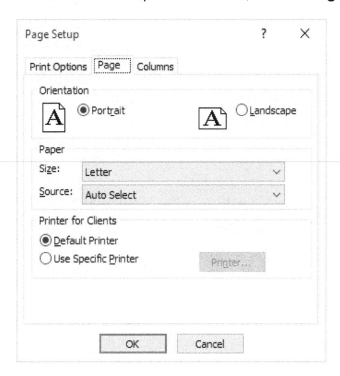

Orientation The page orientation (portrait or landscape) can be changed by clicking/tapping on the appropriate radio button.

Paper Click or tap on the down arrow ⌄ to the right of the "Paper Size" section to select from one of many predefined sizes. You may also select the source (tray) for the paper.

Printer Allows you to specify the printer to be used. Click or tap on Printer... to choose a printer other than the default.

Once settings have been changed, select OK .

CHANGING THE COLUMN LAYOUT

The last tab of the page setup box is used to modify the layout of the columns on the report, as shown below:

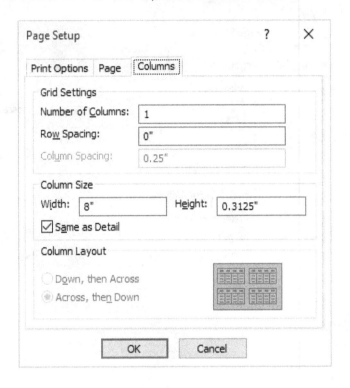

Grid Settings	Use the top section of this tab to specify the number of columns to print on one page and the spacing between rows and/or columns.
Column Size	Use the middle section to specify the width/height of each column.
Column Layout	Use this section to specify if the columns will be printed across then down, or down then across the page.

Once all settings have been changed, select [OK].

PRINTING THE REPORT

Once you have made all your changes and are ready to print the report, follow these steps:

Print

Click or tap on this tool (located within the **Print** section of the Print Preview Ribbon).

The following dialog box will be displayed:

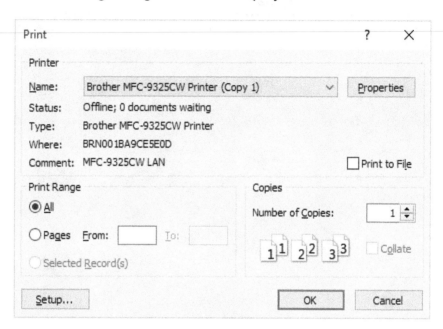

Select the printer, enter the number of copies desired, and select which pages of the report you want printed.

When done, select OK.

PRACTICE EXERCISE

Instructions:	❶	Create a report based on the **Clients** table.
	❷	Create a tabular report using all the fields. The report should be grouped by state and sorted by last names and first names, in that order.
	❸	Print/preview the report and name the report "Client Listing by State".

www.ingramcontent.com/pod-product-compliance
Lightning Source LLC
Chambersburg PA
CBHW060159060326
40690CB00018B/4175